Gamophobia

An Essential Guide to Understanding Why You're Scared to Get Married and How to Overcome Gamophobia

by Deborah Kurtcher

Table of Contents

Introduction

Marriage is a life-changing decision that affects the outcome of the rest of your life, so it's understandable for someone to be apprehensive or experience cold feet as the big day approaches. However, if just the thought of marriage alone sends shivers up your spine, or sends you running for the hills away from every promising relationship, well then, we might be looking at a more complicated problem.

If you haven't heard the germ 'Gamophobia' before, it's just a fancy way of describing the irrational and uncontrollable fear of marriage, and sometimes the fear of commitment in general. Although it may sound silly and like something you can eventually overcome on your own when "the right person" comes along, it is actually a debilitating and destructive condition that needs to be addressed head-on because it may prevent you from ever experiencing the fulfillment and happiness that can accompany an intimate connection and partnership with another person.

You know how some people are afraid of heights, to a degree that just doesn't make sense? For example, some people suffering from this phobia become paralyzed when standing inside a tall building just by looking out the window. The problem of gamophobia is similar in that it's an extreme and irrational version of the fear of marriage. Sometimes, just a single thought of getting married can trigger a real panic attack. In the majority of cases, people even recognize that their fears are illogical, but still, they can't control them because these fears are governed by the unconscious parts of their minds.

If you suffer from this gamophobia and you are in a committed relationship, you are likely to do everything you can to maintain the current status rather than make the decision to tie the knot. Even though things may seem fine to you now, you are probably at least somewhat aware of the potential consequences of your fear. Not only may you experience so many negative feelings and disappointments later in life, but your phobia may influence other people's lives as well – in particular, your significant other's!

It's important to understand that gamophobia is not a rare fear as you might think at first. During the last 15 years, it's actually been increasing, especially among men. Most people are not willing to acknowledge the existence of this fear, whereas others don't even know of its existence in concrete terms.

The good news is, there's a way to overcome this phobia so that the phrase "happily ever after" can finally be applied to you too. Fortunately, as with other known phobias, gamophobia can also be cured with the help of various effective and beneficial techniques.

So whether you are the one suffering from gamophobia or it is your partner, the first step to take in dealing with this problem to educate yourself about the fear, and then develop a game plan of action. And that's exactly what this book is designed to help you get started doing, so get started reading now, and you may soon find yourself a lot more accepting towards the idea of committing yourself to another person by getting married.

Life is not life if you live in fear.

Chapter 1: Understanding What Gamophobia Really Is

Gamophobia typically refers to the irrational and uncontrollable fear of marriage, although some people use this term to refer to the fear of commitment as well. However, some experts believe that a subtle difference between these two may be observed. Namely, a person may be committed to his/her partner despite the fear of getting married.

Even though most people think that gamophobia is not that serious, and that it is the same as having cold feet as your marriage is getting closer, it actually refers to the strong fear that appears at the thought of committing for life. People who experience this kind of fear typically find it more suitable to remain bachelors or spinsters or to stay in a committed relationship than to decide to take their relationship to a higher level.

Gamophobia is a serious thing to consider because it doesn't only impose certain limitations on your life but it may also leave you vulnerable to some psychological disorders, such as, alcohol abuse or depression. It may also affect your relationships with your family, friends, coworkers, relatives, etc. Those who are at a greater risk of developing this kind of fear include people who have a tendency to feel panicky or anxious, those dealing with adrenalin insufficiency or those characterized as nervous, easily upset and energetic.

You may think that this is not such a common phobia, but you are wrong. The symptoms of gamophobia and the feelings that follow them occur very frequently. So, there's no reason to think that there's something wrong with you. It's normal for your brain to create positive and negative emotions and associations with certain concepts. This book will help you learn how to control these associations and turn them to your benefit. You will be surprised how easy it is to banish this phobia for good.

Chapter 2: Recognizing and Identifying the Symptoms

Similar to other phobias, symptoms of gamophobia differ from one person to another, and their intensity depends on the level of fear a person experiences. This is so, simply because the patterns of thinking associated with commitment and marriage, which actually form the essence of the phobia, differ from one person to another. However, it is possible to observe some general symptoms that most people suffering from this type of phobia experience. Since gamophobia, or fear generally, can sometimes be viewed as a physical response to your patterns of thinking, in the case of thinking about marriage and commitment, most people suffering from gamophobia may have really strong reactions to just a thought about the cause of their fear. Some physical symptoms of gamophobia may be so unpleasant that for most people, it may be easier to completely avoid situations that may trigger their fear. The feelings of fear and anxiety may vary from very mild anxiety to severe panic attacks. Usually, as you find yourself closer to your fear, your panic and fear become greater.

All these symptoms may be manifested on the emotional, psychological and physical level, and they all typically show up when the concept of marriage is mentioned.

As for the emotional symptoms, they include the following:

- desire to flee / intense instinct to leave the situation; when you think about marriage and commitment, you are overwhelmed by this feeling that you need to do anything to avoid this.

- overwhelming and persistent fear of marriage and commitment

- persistent worrying about upcoming events which involve marriage and commitment

- most people may also experience elevated levels of fear, sadness, anger, guilt and/or hurt when they think about their bad experiences in the past

The psychological symptoms of gamophobia include:

- feeling of losing control or going crazy

- avoiding the topic

- uncontrollable anxiety; because of this feeling, you may sometimes feel unable to function normally

- feeling terror or dread when thinking about marriage

- the person understands that this fear is irrational but is too powerless to control or overcome it

- fear of fainting

- feelings of being detached from yourself

- bad and negative images of marriage and commitment

- experiencing difficulty thinking about anything other than your fear

- obsessive thoughts

The physical symptoms of gamophobia may be:

- hot or cold flashes

- numbness

- feeling dizzy

- stomach distress or nausea

- sweating

- feeling of choking

- trembling

- chest pain

- pounding heart or accelerated heart rate

- shortness of breath

- crying

Chapter 3: Getting to the Underlying Root Cause

Generally speaking, all phobias arise due to a combination of internal and external factors. Genetics and heredity are considered to be those internal factors which lead to phobias, whereas traumatic experiences or events from the past are typically those external causes of phobias. Even though most phobias can actually be traced back to some specific traumatic experience, which most frequently occurred at an early age, social phobias, where gamophobia may be included as well, are thought to be more complex to explain. Usually, it is believed that they are caused by a combination of genetics and traumatic experiences. This negative experience traumatizes the individuals to such an extent that they dread commitment or marriage. You may now conclude that gamophobia is not an inborn thing. So, just as you may learn it as you grow up, you may also learn how to banish it from your life.

Some people don't even remember the cause of their fear; however, they still experience these gamophobia symptoms. This happens because your brain recognizes certain situations as dangerous, because it finds similarities with some of the previous unpleasant experiences and thus, your brain switches to the so-called fight or flight mode. And that's when

yes *
without
even
realizing
it

17

your heart starts pounding and you feel like running away.

No matter what the cause of your phobia is, it's actually great to know that you don't need to trace it back in order to overcome it. It is more important how you react to your fear, more precisely how your mind reacts—whether it creates still movies or pictures in your mind, you hear some voice in your head, or you are overwhelmed by negative thoughts.

When you come to think how many unsuccessful marriages there are nowadays, you are certain to be disappointed. You have probably witnessed many cases of failed relationships and marriages, and you don't want the same to be the case with you. Thus, you may feel safe if you just avoid being even near that kind of commitment or situation.

However, things are not always as they seem. When you hear about someone's failed marriage, you actually don't ask or want to know the reasons. And reasons may be numerous and various. For instance, it's not a rare case that young people get married because of the upcoming baby. These marriages are often doomed to failure. Just think about it. When these people mature, they realize how different they are from each other and that their goals, hopes and dreams are different to the extent that a divorce is the best solution. Some other marriages may end because one of the partners has got emotionally involved with another person. In some other cases, when children grow up and start their own families, partners may all of a sudden realize that they have grown apart. Domestic violence is another cause for a growing number of divorces. These are some of the possible reasons, although there may be many others. However, the point is that these are all the things which may keep you away from marriage, although none of these things may ever happen to you. It is true that when you read all of these, you don't have any positive opinion about marriage, but these things don't happen to everyone.

If you still don't know whether you're suffering from gamophobia, here's a really short test. Just think about marriage and commitment and answer these questions:

1. Does your heart begin to pound?

2. Do you feel that your mouth is dry?

3. Does this feeling trigger clammy hands?

4. Do you feel dizzy or unable to stand?

5. Do you feel nausea when someone mentions marriage or commitment?

Is your answer to most of these questions "YES?" If it is, go on to the next chapter to read about some possible ways to overcome gamophobia.

Chapter 4: How to Treat Gamophobia

Gamophobia works in such a way that your mind actually triggers the fear when you think of marriage and commitment. So, you need to somehow change these patterns of thinking. Consciously, you know that your fear is illogical. But when you think of marriage, your subconscious mind triggers these negative emotions. You can get rid of these automatic feelings, and it's not a hard thing to do. You will just need to apply the adequate techniques that will help you change your reactions to your triggers.

Some possible ways of treating gamophobia include talk therapy, hypnotherapy, exposure therapy, behavioral, anchoring, medications, and relaxation techniques (visualization and controlled breathing). Are you ready to get started with vanquishing this fear forever?

Talk Therapy

If you think that you can't do it alone and that you need help, you can talk to your GP with a view of finding a specialist in mental health conditions. The results will depend on the type of method as well as on the experience of the person you talk to. You should know that results with this kind of therapy come slowly. With talk therapy, you are encouraged to talk about your fear, but not only about that. You may also talk about different aspects of marriage. This need not be any health or psychological expert, but it is important that this is the person the sufferer can trust. In the beginning, this may be a friend or parent. Depending on the degree of gamophobia, sometimes it is probably best to seek help from an expert psychiatrist.

Hypnotherapy

This therapy can help trace the root causes of your gamophobia. This will then help you unlearn or rationally explain all these negative thoughts and attitudes you have towards marriage.

Behavioral Therapy

Behavioral therapy has been found successful in many cases of treating phobias. It actually involves a one-to-one session with a therapist who is trained in treating phobias. This technique involves exposure to a certain degree. With the help of relaxation techniques, you will learn to tolerate the anxiety that is triggered by this exposure.

The first sessions will involve exposure to not so frightening situations, such as imagining marriage. When your symptoms of gamophobia are triggered, the therapist will guide you to overcome them.

Exposure Therapy

This stems from cognitive-behavioral therapy and involves exposing yourself to stressful situations, which may trigger your fear. The goal is to become familiar with these new situations and be able to overcome your fear successfully. Usually, this involves 5 stages:

- Evaluation—this stage involves talking to your therapist and trying to trace the cause of your fear.

- Feedback—at this stage, your therapist offers a treatment plan.

- Developing fear hierarchy—together with your therapist, and based on what you said about your fear in the first stage, both of you create scenarios that are likely to trigger your fear. This list should include mild to severe situations.

- Exposure—at this stage, you start by exposing yourself to the situations from the list. You will start with the situation that is the least frightening, and you will come to learn that even after a few minutes, your fear lessens.

- Building—once you become comfortable with these not so frightening situations, you can go on to more intense ones.

The good thing about this technique is that it is successful in most cases. It is also important to find an experienced therapist who can be trusted, because you will need to be guided through some very difficult situations. Facing your fear or being exposed to what you are afraid of may be useful in some cases. The idea behind this is that when you are frequently exposed to your fear, or situations that are likely to trigger your fear, you will eventually get used to it and overcome your phobia. However, this is a very unpleasant technique and method for almost all people suffering from any kind of phobia. Moreover, in some cases this is not useful at all, but on the contrary, it may make the phobia worse because you may just reinforce all those negative associations you have about marriage and commitment.

Anchoring

Anchoring is a simple technique and a very effective one which helps with really serious cases of gamophobia.

The first thing to understand is the way in which we create fear in our mind. This actually applies not only to fear, but also to any other feeling you have at any moment in time. This is a result of your physiology and focus. Focus refers to the way you use your mind, more precisely this involves your beliefs as well as the language you use to describe certain things to yourself. On the other hand, your physiology refers to the way you use your body. This includes various things from your breathing and posture to how you drink lots of water for instance. So, every feeling you experience at any time is a result of the combination of these two elements you are using at a given moment. The great news is that when you become able to change the focus and physiology, you will be able to change this feeling as well.

27

Anchoring is based on this—whenever you experience some intense feeling, no matter whether it is pleasant or unpleasant, your mind creates a sort of link between these two—your stimulus and your physical reaction. Let's take this as an example. Do you remember when you first fell in love? Maybe there was some song playing and you associated this song with this feeling of falling in love. Now when you hear that song, this feeling of falling in love comes back to you, right? This link your mind created is actually this anchor—the link between the intense feeling and the unique stimulus.

Now, how will this work with gamophobia? You will need to create a link between some kind of stimulus (and this stimulus should be the one you can control and thus initiate it any time you want) and a mixture of confident and calm emotions with which you want to replace all those negative feelings of gamophobia. Now when you have this new link, whenever you think of marriage, you just need to apply the stimulus and you will experience this new kind of emotion. In other words, your mind will manage to attach positive emotions and replace the old negative ones. So, whenever you find yourself in a situation that is likely to trigger your negative emotions, just rely on your anchor that will help these thoughts of marriage become a neutral and maybe later even a pleasant experience.

It now may seem that this is easier said than done. Here is how to create an anchor:

- Pick the positive emotions you want to anchor. This may be anything you want, such as being totally calm, the feeling of perfect love, excited anticipation, being totally relaxed, etc. It is just important that this is a completely positive and pleasant state of being.

- Choose one unique part of your body to attach this anchor to. For this anchoring to work, you will need a unique stimulus. This stimulus should be something you don't do every day, but also something that you can create easily. There are so many things you can choose, for instance, touching your earlobe, squeezing a tight fist, etc.

- Imagine the situation when you felt that way and allow this positive feeling to flood your body.

- As you feel that your whole body experiences this pleasant feeling, and that it is reaching its peak, press on your anchor for 10 seconds, making sure that your stimulus is unique.

- When you feel that your feelings are at their highest, apply your anchor for 10 seconds. This is an important thing to do because this is when your brain creates the link between the feeling and the stimulus.

- Allow your feelings to return to normal.

- Repeat the same procedure a number of times to make the anchor more powerful and useful. You need to create a strong anchor so that you can use it for longer if needed.

- When you find yourself in challenging situations, fire your anchor.

Gamophobia Medications

Many different types of medications can be used to treat phobias, such as beta-blockers and antidepressants.

- Beta-blockers are used because they can block the flow of adrenaline, which occurs when you are anxious, and thus they also can control some of your physical symptoms, such as sweating, trembling voice or hands, or rapid heartbeat.

- Antidepressants are generally used to treat the feelings of fear.

- Benzodiazepines act really fast and they act as anti-anxiety medications, but they are addictive.

Although medications may seem to offer you a solution, they are not actually a good thing to use. In other words, when you stop using them, your symptoms of gamophobia will certainly return. Don't overlook all the side effects either. The bottom line is that medications can mask the symptoms, but they will never cure the root cause of your phobia. Because of that, using medications and drugs for treating gamophobia is generally not encouraged. In case you take some medications, you should always consult with your doctor if you want to change these, but again, these medications will not deal with the cause of your problem.

Self-Help

Self-help really means that you can do some things by yourself. There's not one unique successful program, but whatever method you choose to deal with your phobia, you need to take responsibility for yourself. This is a recommended technique because you are actually the only one who can manage to break those ties between your fear and marriage.

Relaxation Techniques

Relaxation techniques work well for mild cases of gamophobia, but with people who experience real panic and fear, just remembering how to breathe will not be of much help. Thus, these are successful only with mild cases of gamophobia.

1. Breathing technique for stress relief

This breathing technique focuses on deep and cleansing breaths for a powerful relief from stress. This is easy to learn and you can practice anywhere when in need. The key thing this technique relies on is breathing deeply from your abdomen. This kind of breathing supplies your lungs with more fresh air; and the more oxygen you get, the less anxious you feel. This is how to do it:

- Sit comfortably on the floor or wherever you find suitable, paying attention that your back is straight. Place one hand on your abdomen and another on your chest.

- Inhale through your nose and you will feel how your hand on your stomach rises; feel how your hand on your chest rises just a little.

- Breathe out through your mouth and push as much air as you can from your lungs. You should feel how your hand on your belly moves in, whereas your other hand moves very little.

- Repeat the same procedure until you feel that your whole body is relaxed.

Note: If it is difficult for you to breathe deeply and feel your belly expand, you should try the exercise lying on the floor.

2. Visualization meditation for stress relief

Besides your visual sense, this kind of meditation employs your sense of touch, taste, sound and smell. This technique is aimed at relieving you from all the anxiety and tension you feel. Basically, you need to imagine some scene that is soothing for you. You can do this while listening to some music that matches your scene, or if you prefer, you can do it in silence as well.

To practice this visualization technique, follow these steps:

- Find some quiet place and sit there comfortably, or if you think that you may fall asleep while doing this, you can sit up.

- Close your eyes and imagine some peaceful place. Let your imagination work in its own way, allowing as many images to appear in your mind. You should include all your senses here so that you have as many details as possible about this imaginary place.

- When you employ all your senses, you will feel how this feeling of peace and relaxation floods you.

- When you feel that your whole body is completely relaxed, you can open your eyes.

Note: You may feel sleepy after this technique, but it is normal and it's only a sign that your body is relaxed.

Maybe you have been wondering whether or not you can ever get rid of this fear. If you have read everything carefully so far, you can now come to only this conclusion—if you want to put this behind you once and for all, then you will succeed in doing so.

Chapter 5: Important Advice and Practical Tips

The first step is to accept that nothing is perfect and that life is far away from being a fairy tale. All sorts of problems will arise, but hopefully there is help everywhere, you just need to spot them and open up to them. The only thing certain in this world is that life is full of choices, and you go through life by trying to make the right ones.

Here are some practical tips that may help you solve some problems that may arise in your relationship or future marriage, and which are likely to intensify or trigger your fear.

Are you really ready for marriage?

Maybe your relationship seems to be perfect but there's still something that prevents you from tying the knot. Think about your relationship and about these questions:

- Will you be happier with some other person?

- Is this person the right one for you?

- Are there any other things you need to do before getting married?

- Would you be in love with this person after 20 years?

- Are you ready to fulfill your responsibility as a spouse?

Talk to your partner

Maybe it's hard for you to talk about this with your partner, but you need to. Although you may feel guilty because of your feeling, your partner should not be kept in the dark and deserves to know what is going on with you. Moreover, you can overcome the problem together. This may also help your partner understand some possible causes for your fear and then you may both decide what to do next.

Talk to your parents

If you are not in a relationship, you can talk to other people who know you well. Your parents know your whole childhood and they may help you trace the roots of your problem. In some cases, the reason may be the bad marriage of your parents. If that's the case, your parents may explain to you why their marriage turned out to be that way, which doesn't mean that you will experience that too. If you don't feel like talking to your parents, then talk to your friends instead.

Problem identification

Your marriage won't succeed without lots of effort and work. It's normal that problems may arise occasionally and you know that there's no reason to end your relationship without even considering the problems and attempting to solve them. So, in case you think you may feel unhappy or dissatisfied in marriage, you have to identify the causes of such feelings and then discuss them with your partner.

There's no more thrill

People have different expectations when it comes to marriage. For most of them, marriage is the same as being in a relationship with only one exception—you live in the same house or flat with your partner. Living together with the person you wish to marry to actually involves dealing with all the nitty-gritty of everyday life with that person. Once you get to this point, you'll see how different it is from being in a relationship and how much effort it will take to make your marriage work.

Of course, there will certainly be some things that your partner does that irritate you a lot. On the other hand, don't you think that you also do such things, and that your partner isn't perfectly satisfied with everything you do? However, if both of you know how to say nice things to each other, you will find a way to neglect and not pay attention to these irritating habits. Take this into account as well—when either one or both of you don't have anything nice to say to each other, these annoyances may become far worse than they actually are.

Children?

Maybe you have some conflicting attitudes when it comes to children, such as, how to raise them, wanting similar, if not the same, goals for your children, sharing responsibilities, etc. Make all of these points clear, so that this won't be one of the obstacles to your marriage.

Financial issues may make you fear marriage

There are several things that may cause problems in your marriage when it comes to finances. Maybe one of you wants more of the good life than you two can actually afford, or one of you is too controlling and the other one has a less serious attitude when it comes to your expenditures. Maybe one of you two or both of you have been unemployed for a longe period of time. Does one of you feel inferior because the other makes more money? Financial issues may cause lots of problems indeed but the key thing is again to sit together and talk everything through.

If you have financial problems, you can also consult a financial adviser to end these disputes. He/she will help you create your financial plan, teach you how to stick to it, consolidate debt, and set your budget. Both of you should check in with your financial advisor on a regular basis so that you can get a review of whether or not both you and your partner can live within you income on your own.

Fear of being trapped in an abusive marriage

This point may be the most difficult one to resolve. It has to do with any sort of abuse—emotional, physical, verbal, or sexual. If you are afraid of getting married because some of these can be applied to your partner, then your fear is justifiable. You should never even consider getting married to such a person because, if you get married, it will be even more difficult to free yourself from this. If there are indications that your partner has changed for better, then your relationship may have some future, but if this is not the case, run. According to statistics, domestic violence in the majority of cases gets more severe as time passes.

Treat any existing addictions

Depending on the degree of your gamophobia, sometimes it is best to find a therapist. This is a problem both you and your partner need to solve, therefore, it is advisable to talk to your partner about this and ask him/her to join you in trying to overcome these fears of yours.

Once you get this kind of help, your therapist or councilor may recognize some kind of addiction which prevents you and your partner from having the kind of relationship both of you want. In some cases, even though people recognize they have this kind of problem, they refuse to seek help for various reasons. So, if you are the one whose partner has this marriage fear, be prepared, because you may need lots of effort and patience to get your partner to the point of recognizing the need for help. You may also try to get parents or friends to talk your partner into seeking help.

Conclusion

Since you read this far, chances are you or someone you know has experienced living with the symptoms and effects of gamophobia. By following the effective methods in this book though, you can finally overcome this fear and leave it behind you. You deserve to have the kind of fulfilled life that you want to have with no limitations and obstacles. All relationships have ups and downs, but when you finally banish irrational fears, you will suddenly realize all those wonderful things about marriage that you didn't notice before. I hope you will apply the techniques presented in this book and take the first steps towards your happiness.

Finally, I'd like to thank you for purchasing this book! If you found it helpful, I'd greatly appreciate it if you'd take a moment to leave a review on Amazon. Thank you!

Made in the USA
Columbia, SC
10 September 2020